THIS LAND CALLED AMERICA: ILLINOIS

CREATIVE EDUCATION

Published by Creative Education
P.O. Box 227, Mankato, Minnesota 56002
Creative Education is an imprint of The Creative Company
www.thecreativecompany.us

Book and cover design by Blue Design (www.bluedes.com)
Art direction by Rita Marshall
Printed in the United States of America

Photographs by Alamy (Danita Delimont), Corbis (Tom Bean, Bett-
mann, Sandy Felsenthal, Thomas A. Heinz, Lake County Museum, David
Muench, Reuters), Getty Images (ARCHIVE PHOTOS, George Catlin,
H. T. Cory/National Archives/Time Life Pictures, Gordon Coster//
Time Life Pictures, Robert Francis, STAN HONDA/AFP, Adam Lubroth,
Francis Miller//Time Life Pictures, MPI, B. Anthony Stewart, UNIVER-
SITY/AFP, Tom Vezo, Konrad Wothe)

Library of Congress Cataloging-in-Publication Data
Shofner, Shawndra.
Illinois / by Shawndra Shofner.
p. cm. — (This land called America)
Includes bibliographical references and index.
ISBN 978-1-58341-638-9
1. Illinois—Juvenile literature. I. Title. II. Series.
F541.3.S52 2008
977.3—dc22   200715006

First Edition
9 8 7 6 5 4 3 2 1

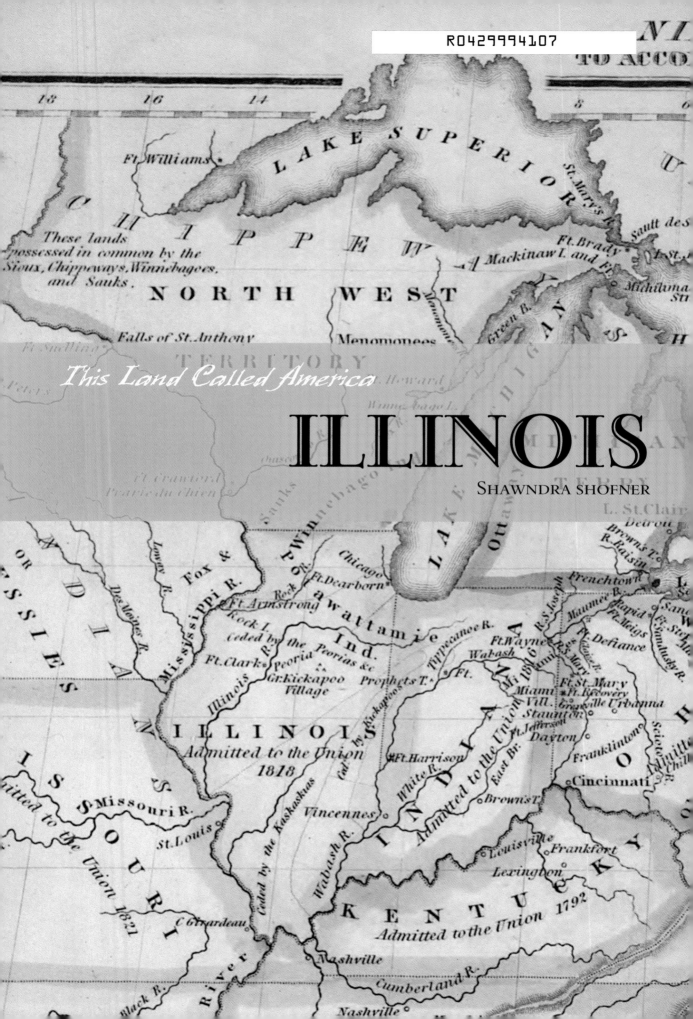

This Land Called America

ILLINOIS

Shawndra shofner

Illinois

SHAWNDRA SHOFNER

THE EARLY MORNING SUN SHINES ON A SMALL
FARM. ON THIS WARM SPRING DAY IN ARTHUR,
ILLINOIS, A WOMAN WEARING A FULL SKIRT, WOOL
CAPE, AND BLACK BONNET HANGS SHEETS ON
THE CLOTHESLINE. TWO YOUNG GIRLS, DRESSED
LIKE THEIR MOTHER, WASH WINDOWS. IN THE
DISTANCE, THEIR FATHER GUIDES A HORSE-DRAWN
PLOW THROUGH THE FIELD. HE IS PREPARING
THE GROUND FOR A CROP OF CORN. AMID THE
FACTORIES AND CITIES OF URBAN ILLINOIS, MORE
THAN 4,500 AMISH PEOPLE STILL LIVE IN MUCH
THE SAME WAY TODAY AS DID THEIR ANCESTORS
WHO FIRST SETTLED IN THE EAST-CENTRAL PART
OF THE STATE IN 1865.

YEAR
1673
EVENT

Explorers Louis Jolliet and Jacques Marquette first travel into the land of Illinois.

Early Illinoisans

AMERICAN INDIANS WERE THE FIRST PEOPLE TO LIVE IN
THE FORESTS AND PRAIRIES OF ILLINOIS. THEY HUNTED
BEAR, DEER, AND BUFFALO. FROM FLOWING RIVERS, THEY
TRAPPED BEAVERS, MUSKRATS, AND OTTERS. THEY GREW
CORN AND SQUASH, AND THEY GATHERED NUTS AND
FRUIT, SUCH AS PECANS AND PLUMS, FROM TREES.

French explorers Jacques Marquette and Louis Jolliet canoed down the Mississippi River in 1673. They met tribes of friendly Indians who called themselves "Illini." The Illini showed the explorers how to get back north to Lake Michigan and Canada by traveling up the Illinois and Des Plaines rivers, carrying their canoes over land, and continuing up the Chicago River.

Just as they had helped French explorers in the mid-1600s (opposite), Indians again came to the aid of the French during the French and Indian Wars (above).

In 1682, another French explorer, René-Robert de La Salle, traveled from Canada to the Gulf of Mexico. He claimed Illinois for France, along with all land west of the Mississippi River to the Rocky Mountains and north from the Gulf of

YEAR
1778
EVENT
American general George Rogers Clark leads a surprise attack and defeats English soldiers at Kaskaskia.

- 7 -

D Hartley

John Adams.

B Franklin

John Jay

Mexico to Canada. He named the vast territory Louisiana after France's King Louis XIV.

France and England both wanted control of the profitable fur trade in North America. In the French and Indian Wars of 1754–1763, some Indians fought alongside French soldiers to keep the English from taking over their land. But England won and claimed most of France's land in North America, including Illinois.

England's King George III, who also ruled over the 13 American colonies, made a law in 1763 that no people could settle west of the Appalachian Mountains. But many colonists wanted to explore lands such as Illinois. This was one of many disputes between the colonists and England that led to the Revolutionary War in 1775.

Although most of the war was fought within the colonies, English forts in Illinois were also raided by colonists in the late 1770s. England lost the war, and lands west and north of the Ohio River, including present-day Illinois, became part of the United States' Northwest Territory in 1787. Colonists from Kentucky, Virginia, and Missouri quickly settled in the open lands of Illinois.

American politicians such as John Adams signed a document to end the Revolutionary War in 1783.

In 1809, Illinois became a U.S. territory. The territory included land that would become the states of Illinois, Wisconsin, Minnesota, and Michigan. Nine years later, on December

YEAR

1800   The Northwest Territory is divided, and Illinois becomes part of the Indiana Territory.

EVENT

- 9 -

Young Abraham Lincoln never saw active combat or met Chief Black Hawk (below), but he visited the battlefields of the Civil War as president (opposite).

3, 1818, Illinois became the 21st state in America.

As more white people moved into Illinois, American Indians were forced out of the way. Some tried to resist. Chief Black Hawk led 400 Sauk and Fox Indians in battles against Illinois settlers in April 1832. Governor John Reynolds sent in 1,600 troops to protect the settlers. The Black Hawk War ended with Black Hawk's capture in August, resulting in a peace treaty in September.

Abraham Lincoln was a young captain in the Black Hawk War. His family had moved to Illinois in 1830. After the war, he served in the state legislature and the U.S. Congress before becoming the country's 16th president in 1861. Even before Lincoln took office, seven Southern states left the Union because they were afraid he would free the South's slaves. They were joined by four more states. This started the Civil War. More than 250,000 troops from Illinois fought for the Union, or North, during the bloody war. General Ulysses S. Grant, from Galena, Illinois, helped the Union win the war in 1865.

YEAR

1818 Illinois is admitted as the 21st state on December 3.

EVENT

The Prairie State

Five states surround the midwestern state of Illinois. The northwestern corner of Kentucky forms the southern border. The Wabash River makes up about half of the eastern border with Indiana, while the Mississippi River runs along the western border with Missouri and Iowa.

Big sheets of ice called glaciers flattened much of the land as they moved through Illinois thousands of years ago. The state gets its nickname as "The Prairie State" from the vast prairies of windswept grasses and flowers that once covered more than 60 percent of the land. That flat, fertile land attracted many of the state's first white settlers. They plowed the prairies and planted large fields of corn and soybeans. Even though most of the prairie in Illinois is now farmed, more than 200 protected prairie sites exist in the state.

A 1940s postcard from Starved Rock State Park highlighted the many natural features within the park.

There are three main types of prairie in North America: tallgrass (found in Illinois), mixed-grass, and shortgrass.

In contrast to the prairies of central Illinois, canyons, bluffs, and large rocks line the Illinois River in the northwest. This beautiful area near Utica is protected as Starved Rock State Park. Rushing waterfalls flow from 18 canyons in the spring. Wood ducks, beavers, and muskrats swim in the water. Yellowbellied sapsuckers feed on sap from cedar trees on the bluffs. Birds such as cedar waxwings flutter and feed among serviceberry and honeysuckle bushes. Red oak and hickory trees provide shade to ferns, huckleberries, and witch hazel.

YEAR

1827 The first college in Illinois, Rock Spring Seminary, opens in Mount Morris.

EVENT

The Shawnee Hills lie between the Mississippi and Ohio rivers on the state's southern edge. Maple, dogwood, beech, and oak trees fill the rough and rugged Shawnee National Forest. In its Garden of the Gods, one can find unusual rock formations in the shapes of such things as a monkey's head and a camel. White-tailed deer, wild turkey, and Canada geese call this area home. Unusual plants and animals, including the whorled pogonia orchid, Indiana bat, and scarlet tanager still thrive there.

More than 500 rivers and streams wind through Illinois. Most of them flow to the Mississippi. The Chicago and Calumet rivers flowed to Lake Michigan until the early 1900s.

The scarlet tanager (above), which is native to the eastern U.S., can be found in Illinois' Shawnee National Forest, which also contains the rocky Garden of the Gods (opposite).

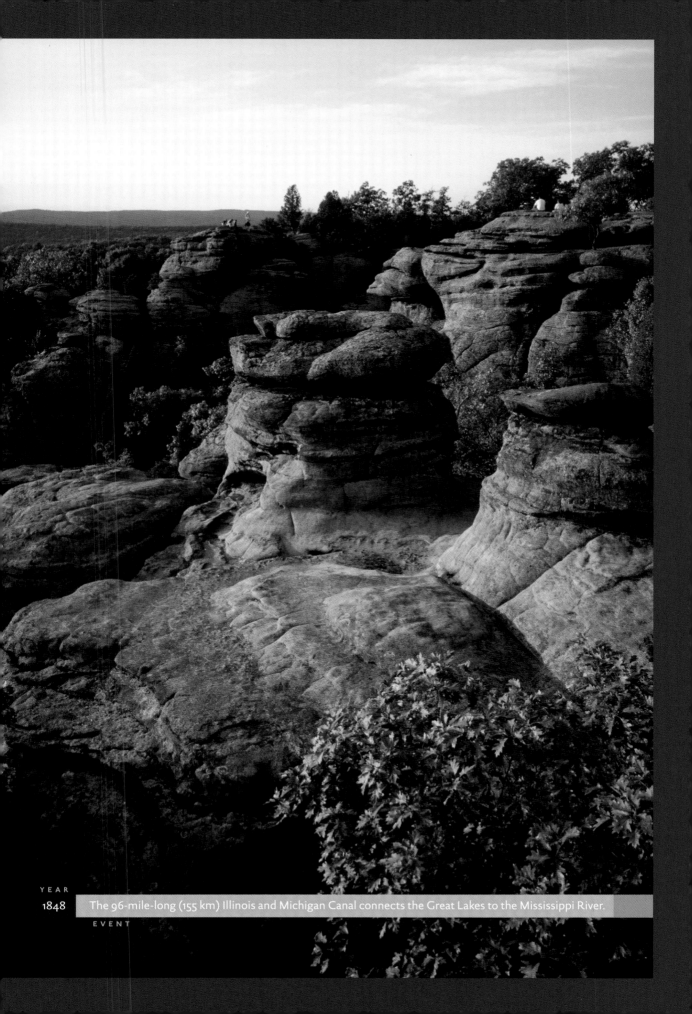

YEAR
1848
EVENT

The 96-mile-long (155 km) Illinois and Michigan Canal connects the Great Lakes to the Mississippi River.

The number of dairy farms in Illinois has been decreasing in recent years due to sell-offs to bigger operations.

Coal miners work underground for long stretches of time and get very dirty from the coal dust.

Then workers built canals that forced the rivers to flow in reverse to the Mississippi River. People use the waterways of Illinois for business and recreation.

Farming takes up most of the land in Illinois. Many farmers grow soybeans, corn, or wheat. Others grow fruits such as apples, raspberries, or peaches. Hog, cattle, and dairy farms are scattered throughout Illinois as well. Some natural resources come from under the ground. Illinois is second only to Montana in coal production among the states. People in Illinois also mine for lead, zinc, and silica sand, the last of which is used to make glass.

Illinois gets a taste of all four seasons. People in the north often endure blizzards in the winter. A seven-day snowstorm in January 1967 dumped 23 inches (58 cm) of snow in the Chicago area. Average temperatures in January are 26 °F (-3 °C). When spring comes, so do floods, windstorms, thunderstorms, and tornadoes. About 38 inches (97 cm) of rain and snow fall every year in the state. Once in a while, a long stretch of hot, dry weather, or drought, affects Illinois. The most recent drought happened in 2005. Many fields dried up, and crops died. In July, temperatures usually average near 76 °F (24 °C).

Illinois dairy farm

YEAR

1861   Illinois senator Abraham Lincoln becomes the 16th president of the U.S.

EVENT

Great Migrations

The French were the first white people to settle in Illinois. They lived in small villages along the rivers. After the American colonists won the Revolutionary War, people from the eastern states came to Illinois in search of cheap farmland. By the 1850s, many German and Swedish people had immigrated to the prairie to farm as well.

The long-held customs of Chicago's large Polish community have contributed to the city's diversity.

Jobs in coal mines and factories attracted many people from Poland, Ukraine, and other eastern European countries in the early 1900s. People from China, Vietnam, and Korea came to Illinois after World War II and the Vietnam War. Mexicans, Cubans, and Venezuelans are among those who have emigrated in recent years. People move to Illinois every day because of its variety of cultures and job opportunities.

African Americans left the South in the 1870s following the Civil War and later in the 1900s.

More than one million African Americans left their homes in the South between 1914 and 1950. They were tired of being mistreated by white people, and they wanted different jobs. This event was called the Great Migration. Thousands of

African Americans rode the Illinois Central Railroad to a neighborhood of Chicago called South Side. This community is known for its many jazz clubs. Famous clarinet player Benny Goodman grew up in Chicago. He was nicknamed the "King of Swing" for his upbeat, swinging jazz music. His band toured the country and, in New York City in 1938, played Carnegie Hall's first jazz concert.

Of the states in the Midwest, Illinois has the greatest population: 12,831,970 people. While around five million people live in Illinois' rural areas, almost three million live in its biggest city, Chicago. Almost another six million live in the suburbs surrounding the "Windy City."

People from all corners of the world live in Chicago. Many work in medical, financial, or educational jobs. In addition to its bustling downtown and miles of suburbs, the city contains 77 large ethnic neighborhoods. These communities were each settled by immigrants with similar backgrounds. Many Chinese and Vietnamese live in Chinatown. In Rogers Park, Pakistanis and Russians mingle. Visitors and residents enjoy the variety of culture, food, and art found in these unique neighborhoods.

More than 80 percent of the land in Illinois is used for farming. But only 1 out of every 50 workers in Illinois is a farmer. The first manufacturing industries in Illinois came

Benny Goodman and his orchestra

YEAR
1871 The Great Chicago Fire kills more than 300 people and leaves another 100,000 without homes.
EVENT

Young people enjoyed listening to Benny Goodman, the "King of Swing," play his clarinet in the 1930s.

YEAR

1906   The Chicago White Sox defeat the Chicago Cubs to win baseball's World Series.

EVENT

- 21 -

about to help make farming easier. Plows that farmers brought with them when they migrated from the East did not work well in the sticky, root-clumped ground of the prairie.

An Illinois blacksmith named John Deere from Grand Decatur solved the problem. In 1837, he invented a steel plow that easily cut through the land. Ten years later, the International Harvester Company in Chicago was started by Cyrus McCormick. He and his father invented the horse-drawn mechanical reaper. This machine helped farmers harvest their crops more quickly.

By the early 1900s, McCormick had become a well-known and reliable brand of farming equipment.

YEAR

1926   Pilot Charles Lindbergh starts delivering mail on daily flights between Chicago and St. Louis.

EVENT

M
any well-known retail stores got their start in Illinois. Merchant Marshall Field opened Chicago's first department store in 1881. Large catalog retailers Montgomery Ward and Sears were also launched in Illinois. Charles Walgreen was born near Galesburg, Illinois. After losing a finger in a shoe factory accident, Walgreen trained to become a pharmacist. His drugstores were the first to feature lunch counters and soda fountains.

Begun as a mail-order jeweler in Minneapolis, retailer Sears (opposite) moved to Chicago in 1893 and soon rivaled Marshall Field's (above).

Milk-shake-mixer salesman Ray Kroc opens the first McDonald's fast-food restaurant in Des Plaines.

Midwest Marvels

The largest ancient Native American city in the U.S. is preserved at Cahokia, Illinois. Up to 20,000 people lived at the 4,000-acre (1,619 ha) site from a.d. 700 to 1400. Dominating the site is the 100-foot-tall (30 m) Monk's Mound, which got its name from a group of Irish Catholic monks that lived nearby in 1810. Its base is bigger than Egypt's Great Pyramid of Giza.

A more recent architect left his mark on Illinois as well. Oak Park is home to the world's largest collection of Prairie Style houses and buildings designed by Frank Lloyd Wright. He made use of inside light and open spaces in buildings that hugged the ground and had sloping roofs. The house Wright designed for Chicago businessman Frederick C. Robie in 1908 changed architecture forever. With its distinctive horizontal lines, overhangs, and open spaces, the home is still considered an architectural masterpiece.

Chicago's Sears Tower, completed in 1973, is the fourth-tallest building in the world. The skyscraper's spire is a quarter of a mile (442 m) above the ground. Every year, about 1.3 million tourists ride an elevator up 103 floors to visit the Skydeck observatory. On a clear day, people can see as far away as 50 miles (80 km), glimpsing views of Michigan, Indiana, and Wisconsin.

After pesticides were banned in the mid-1900s, Griggsville manufacturer J. L. Wade came up with another way to control mosquitoes and other flying pests. He noted that Griggsville was in the migration path of the purple martin, a bird that can eat thousands of insects. So he turned his antenna factory into one that built birdhouses. The purple martins moved in, and the insect population shrank. Today, there are more than

Today, visitors can pay to tour the Robie House, designed by Frank Lloyd Wright.

5,000 birdhouses in Griggsville. The city's tallest birdhouse is 70 feet (21 m) tall with 562 separate apartments.

Robert Pershing Wadlow was born in the western town of Alton in 1918. He started out as a baby of normal size, but he grew faster, taller, and bigger than children his age. By the time he was 13 years old, he was more than seven feet (2 m) tall. He grew to be 8-foot-11 (2.7 m) and 490 pounds (222 kg). Known as the "Gentle Giant," he took the record as the world's biggest man. Wadlow worked as a spokesperson for a shoe company, which gave him his special size 37 shoes. To commemorate its hometown record-holder, a life-size bronze statue was erected at Alton's Southern Illinois University School of Dental Medicine in 1985.

Sports teams from Illinois are known worldwide. Athletes from the University of Illinois at Urbana-Champaign are called the Fighting Illini. Illinois has six professional sports

The Chicago Bulls featured the most famous basketball star of the 1980s and '90s in Michael Jordan.

YEAR

1973   Chicago's Sears Tower opens; it is the tallest building in the world at the time.

EVENT

- 28 -

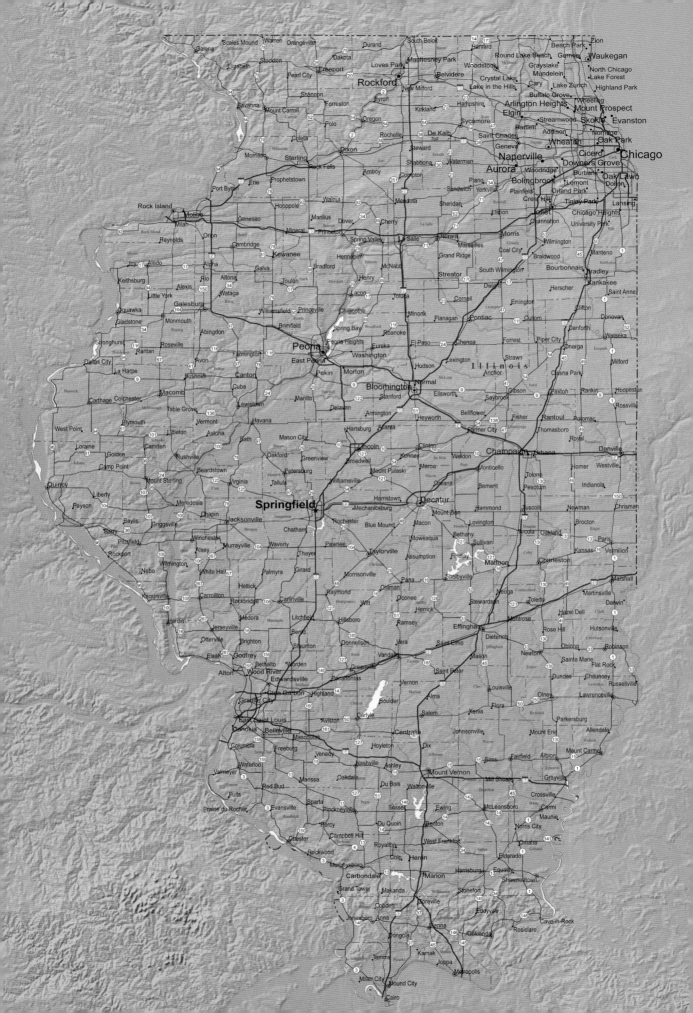

QUICK FACTS

Population: 12,831,970

Largest city: Chicago (pop. 2,869,121)

Capital: Springfield

Entered the union: December 3, 1818

Nickname: Land of Lincoln, Prairie State

State flower: violet

State bird: cardinal

Size: 57,914 sq mi (149,997 sq km)—25th-biggest in U.S.

Major industries: agriculture, finance, manufacturing, technology

teams as well: the National Football League's Chicago Bears, the National Hockey League's Chicago Blackhawks, the National Basketball Association's Chicago Bulls, Major League Baseball's Chicago Cubs and Chicago White Sox, and Major League Soccer's Chicago Fire. The Bears and Bulls have each won many world championships.

Amazing cultural sites, thrilling sports choices, and big-city life are some of the many attractions of Illinois. Its diverse population displays the same strengths as its first pioneers. With so much to offer, it's no wonder that people from around the globe love life on the prairie of Illinois.

Downtown Chicago is known for its many towering skyscrapers, which create a colorful skyline at night.

YEAR 2000 EVENT Chicago's Field Museum of Natural History displays the first nearly complete Tyrannosaurus Rex skeleton.

BIBLIOGRAPHY

Bockenhauer, Mark H., and Stephen F. Cunha. *Our Fifty States*. Washington: National Geographic Society, 2004.

Kaercher, Dan. *Best of the Midwest: Rediscovering America's Heartland*. Guilford, Conn.: Globe Pequot Press, 2005.

Kummer, Patricia K. *Illinois*. Mankato, Minn.: Capstone Press, 2003.

Marshall, Richard, et al. *Explore America*. Washington, D.C.: AAA Publishing, 1996.

Santella, Andrew. *Illinois*. Chicago: Children's Press, 1998.

White, Horace. "The Great Chicago Fire." The National Center for Public Policy Research: Historic Documents. http://www.nationalcenter.org/ChicagoFire.html.

INDEX